GRIEF GUIDE

When a Loved One Dies...

CHAPLAIN KEN RICE

Author's Tranquility Press
ATLANTA, GEORGIA

Chaplain Ken Rice/Author's Tranquility Press
3900 N Commerce Dr. Suite 300 #1255
Atlanta, GA 30344
www.authorstranquilitypress.com

Ordering Information:
Quantity sales. Special discounts are available on quantity purchases by corporations, associations, and others. For details, contact the "Special Sales Department" at the address above.

Grief Guide / Chaplain Ken Rice
Hardback: 978-1-963636-26-0
Paperback: 978-1-963636-27-7
eBook: 978-1-963636-28-4

Contents

DEDICATION

This book is dedicated to those experiencing emotional distress following a loved one's death. The loss of a loved one is something we all go through. From my heart to yours, there is a road to hope, peace, recovery and adaptation for you in *Grief Guide, When a Loved One Dies…*

I am grateful to my wife and best friend, Melissa, for her suggestions and help in editing this book, and for support of my counseling and chaplain ministries. She has been the love of my life for over three decades.

ENDORSEMENTS/REVIEWS

"Ken Rice has provided us with a much-needed resource in his new book, *Grief Guide*. I am confident that the reader will find hope and peace and will be facilitated to the other side of bereavement. This guide has the great benefit of being both brief and yet comprehensive to better serve one in the midst of grief. I am particularly encouraged by the Christ centered message as the distinctive foundation for our hope and peace in this life and life to come. I will eagerly recommend this book to my students in seminary training as well as to others I encounter in ministry."

—Dr. Gary Barnes, ThM, PhD,
Professor of Biblical Counseling,
Dallas Theological Seminary

"What a valuable help your Grief Guide was to me. It covers a wide spectrum of losses, everything from the loss of a spouse to the loss of a child. I appreciated your discussion of emotions and especially the Scriptures you offered for stressful seasons. The clarity with which you presented the gospel was most encouraging, because when it's all said and done, the real comfort comes from knowing that your loved one is at home with the Lord. Good job, Ken, and thank you!"

—Dr. foe Allen Jr., DMin,
Southeastern Baptist Theological Seminary, ThM,
Dallas Theological Seminary, where he serves as the Chaplain

"Ken Rice explores the most basic of human emotions: grief. The brief, easy to read, and readily applicable suggestions are exactly what a hurting person or caregiver needs!"

—Stan Giles, ThM, Dallas Theological Seminary,
United States Air Force Chaplain, Louisville, Tennessee

"I have witnessed Chaplain Rice providing comfort and continued reassurance to the families, friends and coworkers who are experiencing the emotional roller coaster of losing a loved one and fellow firefighter who has died tragically in the line-of-duty. The application of the information provided in Grief Guide works universally and is a constant companion of strength for those seeking understanding and guidance during the difficult time of loss and questioning."

—Robert H. Brown (Retired), Fire Chief,
West Metro Fire Rescue,
Coordinator of the state's team for
line-of duty deaths in Colorado.

"*Grief Guide* is a comprehensive, well written guide which I believe speaks with sensitivity, clarity and honesty in coping with the loss of a loved one. The topics covered are focused not only on helping to better understand the grieving process, but most importantly, provide insight on what bereavement therapy and support may be of value."

—Dave Parmley (Retired), Fire Chief, Lake Dillon Fire
Protection District, Silverthorne, Colorado

"Chaplain Ken has very caringly taken us all on a journey through experiencing and dealing with our own, or our loved ones, process of grieving over the loss of a loved one. He has better prepared us for the day and situation that each one will need to deal with in the not-so-distant future."

—Bruce Mygatt, Fire Chief Boulder Rural Fire Rescue,
Boulder, Colorado

Prelude

"The bustle in a house the morning after death
Is solemnest of industries enacted upon earth—
The sweeping up the heart, and putting love away
We shall not want to use again until eternity."
—Emily Dickinson, 1830-1886

"The joy of our heart has ceased;
Our dance has turned into mourning.

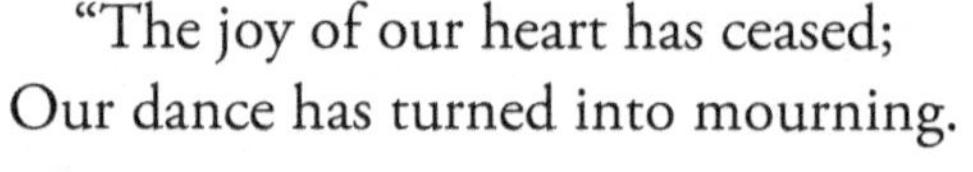

Turn us back to You, O LORD,
And we will be restored;
Renew our days as of old."
—Lamentations 5:15, 21

Like a GPS navigational device, Grief Guide can guide your through the maze of bereavement distress. Your pain does not have to linger for an inordinate amount of time.

My goals are to achieve the following.

- Help you find hope and peace
- Accelerate recovery and adaptation
- Guide you to the outside of bereavement

Attainment of these goals can result in serene life with sunshine breaking through emotionally overcast skies. To help accomplish this, Grief Guide includes a confluence of psychology and theology not generally found in books on bereavement.

May God bless your journey! I would love to hear from you. Email me at: kenrice@reagan.com

In the back of the book, there is a place to record your notes and memories. Information about the author is on the back cover.

The First days Following a Death

When a loved one dies suddenly and unexpectedly, the initial shock and disbelief tend to numb the onset of emotional trauma by momentarily blocking the brain from processing what has happened. Clarity of thought and the ability to remember what you read or hear is temporarily diminished. This serves to slow down the onset of grief. It is like having a *physical* injury causing the body to temporarily go into shock, mitigating and delaying the onset of *physical* pain.

Before reading beyond this chapter, it is recommended that you wait at least twenty-four to forty-eight hours after the death. Some emotional and mental processing time is needed to enable you to think more clearly and remember things better. While you do not need a lot of conversation during this time, you *do* need companionship.

If your loved one lived with you, leave his or her clothing and other personal effects in place to provide a sense of presence. You will know when the time is right to remove certain items. Avoid making significant life changes for a year or two if possible.

If your loved one died as a hospice patient or because of a terminal illness, you can expect to be better prepared emotionally and otherwise. Following the death, grief can be accompanied by a sense of relief that you no longer see your loved one suffering and special care is no longer needed. If this describes your situation, you may not need to delay reading beyond this chapter as suggested for those who lost a loved one suddenly and unexpectedly.

Family dynamics can become complicated and challenging when dealing with end-of-life care and arrangements following the death. Applicable laws are not the same in every state, but generally, if the decedent did not leave written instructions, those having legal decision-making authority are adults in the following order, court-appointed guardian, spouse, sons and daughters, parents, brothers and sisters, other relatives and close friends. It is important for everyone to be sensitive to the feelings of others and to treat each other with understanding, compassion, and respect.

GPS Navigation through Grief and Loss

A GPS (global positioning system) is found in some cars and smartphones for guidance to selected destinations. This book is written to be your GPS for guidance through the maze of grief. It can be a long, difficult, and confusing journey. When we really do not know the way, we let a GPS guide us. It can provide the best route.

To get through bereavement you must go *through* it (not around it). This can take a year, more or less, and there may be obstacles along the way. Sometimes when I end up in an unfamiliar place and want to go home, I simply press the GPS "Home" button. You may discover certain things in this book that are especially helpful to you. Mark them. They could become your "Home" buttons for things to review and repeat along the way.

Introduction to the Bereavement

Bereavement can be defined as the combination of grief and loss. The death of a loved one is a heart-sobering moment for survivors and can be life's most difficult event to deal with. The absence hurts and can produce the deepest sorrow—that hole in your heart. Present expectations may be damaged. The future might seem lost, but it can be reshaped. A positive vista can promote peace.

When in distress, we look and listen but our ability to see and hear (perceive and understand) is subtly impaired. Confusion rules the day. Too often that's why emotional pain and suffering are prolonged and counseling can be so helpful. Grief Guide can help but may not cover certain personal issues—a reason to consider bereavement counseling.

Counseling therapy needs to be done on your terms and when you are ready, with the caveat that action on your part is required. The direction and pace of resolution is up to you.

You may wonder what your emotional journey will be like—how long it will last, how will it affect you, and what the best coping practices are. Answers are here. If grief is not dealt with properly, it can lead to mental and physical health issues. **You will find it beneficial to occasionally review pertinent parts of Grief Guide. At some statements, it can be helpful to pause and ponder.**

Here is an unsolicited excerpt from what a client wrote to me, "Dear Ken, just a little note to say thanks for meeting with me and listening to my grief journey I'm on. You were such a good listener and I appreciate your advice. I read the material you gave me & that is very helpful as well."

Some of the information you are about to read was gleaned from clients who have been there. If you have questions or comments, please feel free to contact me. Your input could be helpful. Thank you. I wish you peace, hope, and well-being.

The "Why" Question

This question sometimes surfaces, especially following the death of a young person. "*Why* did God let this happen?" The answer may lie beyond what you can see at this time and can be like trying to find a few scattered pixels on an IMAX movie screen. It may never be fully understood in this life.

It can seem as though heaven and hell participated in the same event albeit for different reasons. Our faith is sometimes tested. Our ability to function may not be up to par for a while. When life is difficult, we need to trust in God's sovereignty and grace. Accept the fact that there are things our finite minds cannot comprehend. Sometimes life is like a mystery movie that we cannot figure out until the very end.

Many years ago, I had a stillborn son. At the time, even with an incredible sense of peace from the Heavenly Father, I did not understand why He let this happen. There has never been a loss of assurance, however, that I will see my son someday.

The Emotional Journey

It has been said that life is made up of about 10% of what happens to us and 90% of how we react to it. What you are experiencing can have a positive or negative impact on you—better or bitter. Adversity can be a profound teacher and ultimately enrich our lives. Our focus is sharpened and the frivolous weeded out. Emotional valleys can gradually morph into mountains with beautiful life vistas. Your *choice* of attitude and action is now one of the most strategic determinations you can make.

Randy Pausch (1960-2008), an American professor and the author of *The Last Lecture,* was diagnosed with pancreatic cancer and was interviewed on TV about his imminent death. He explained, "We can't change the cards we are dealt, only how we play the hand." We all die, but in the meantime, do we all *really* live?

We do not come equipped with an instant On/Off switch for our emotions, nor do we have soothing background music in real life. So, when does the emotional pain go away? That's akin to asking, "At what time does it become light in the morning?" All we know is that at one time it is dark and later it is light.

The normal decline of death's sting is likewise subtly gradual with no timetable. We tend to shut down and go forward, at least for a while. That hole in your heart can heal. Grief is not an epiphany. It is a natural process of affirmation, resolution, and reconstruction of your life. Don't subdue it; go through it to get through it. *Walk toward the pain.*

The "normal" grief journey can be likened to a scar caused by a wound. The scar remains but fades as it heals. Eventually you seldom notice or think about it. Scar tissue is thicker than normal skin tissue and can provide added resiliency to future wounds. We must adapt when wounds do not fully heal. Consider the life your loved one would want for you going forward. What would he or she say about the life wished for you? Keep the faith; have hope.

Following a close relationship with the decedent, grief typically takes a year or two to resolve, sometimes longer if death occurred under unusual or extraordinary circumstances. Grief may also be prolonged if there is no funeral or memorial service to accelerate closure to the pain.

Avoid interrupting the grief process early on and putting it on hold. Interruptions include significant life changes or events such as removing your loved one's clothing and other personal effects too soon, relocating, changing jobs or careers, having a new intimate relationship, or anything else that pushes the button on the life you were familiar with.

If change results in separation distress, seek counseling to help resolve unfinished emotional business that can return years later. I have counseled those who lost a loved one more than ten years earlier. Their grief process was interrupted and returned later in need of completion.

Consider three questions: (1) Emotionally, where was I prior to the death? (2) Where am I now? (3) Where do I want to be?

Avoidance by Friends Phenomenon

As friends gave you hugs and shook your hand before leaving the funeral or memorial service, you may have heard repeatedly, "If there is anything I can do...." Sometimes later you may notice some of those friends avoiding you.

This is common; here's why. It's not that they don't want to help and show compassion but that they may not know what to say or do. This makes them feel awkward and uncomfortable around you. Also, they "don't want to bother you."

Further, they may feel that your traumatic experience has a contagious nature. To some extent, vicariously it might. But this can help equip *them* with empathy. Those closest to you are simply not always up to the task. Be *forgiving* and help those who should help you.

Let them know *how* they might help you. Tell them, "I need to talk." Mention that just spending a little time with you would be meaningful. If invited, their comfort level increases, and avoidance tends to decrease.

Some well-meaning friends may give advice that is glib, impersonal, and just not helpful like, "Don't cry" or "Just don't think about it" or "Get over it!" Try to ignore those messages and appreciate the fact that they are making themselves available.

You may receive support from those you least expect. Maintain a pleasant attitude that makes them feel comfortable and welcome to come back. In other words, express gratitude and show appreciation.

Sometimes just being with you is enough, especially when friends can't improve on silence. (There appears to be a good reason why we are given two ears but only one mouth.)

Emotional Roller Coaster Reactions

Grief reactions do not abate in a straight line. While they trend downward, reactions are more like a roller coaster, up and down—good days and bad days—rather than going through sequential phases or stages one at a time.

Each of us grieves in a very personal way. Your grief and reactions are as unique to you as your fingerprints. Emptiness and loss are normal predominant feelings. Grief that is moving and changing is good grief. Constant changes signal that you are on the right track and not stuck.

We struggle to live with grief until we can live above it. A study of 233 adults over a two-year period following the loss of a loved one was published in the Journal of the American Medical Association, February 2007. The following findings are general and will not necessarily match your experience. In fact, you might not experience all the following reactions.

The study shows the following: Disbelief peaks about a month after the loss and then declines. It can seem like you are having a nightmare and can't wake up. Emotional distress can impede processing and recording by the brain.

Yearning/longing is when you desperately want your loved one to show up, to walk through the door. This steadily increases and reaches its high point at four months before declining.

Anger rises to a peak at five months. Survivors may struggle with anger escalated by confusion and frustration. Some blame others and become angry with doctors, nurses, relatives, and even resent their loved one for leaving. Some become angry with God. Deal with anger and blame. If needed, try forgiveness. If you have anger, it is helpful to acknowledge your anger.

Depression peaks at six months. After a year, if difficulty coping is constant rather than cyclical, it may indicate one or more depressive disorders—bumps and potholes in the road to recovery. We all occasionally have a "bad day," but if you experience a few of the following symptoms most of *every day* for at least two weeks, get help through counseling:

- Sadness
- Hopelessness
- Pessimism
- Irritability
- Insomnia or oversleeping
- Fatigue
- Feeling worthless or guilty for no reason
- Anorexia or binge eating
- Significant weight change
- Headaches
- Digestive Issues
- Difficulty concentrating
- Suicidal thoughts
- Loss of interest in favorite things

Do not ignore the signs. Failure to recognize symptoms caused by emotional disturbance can result in delayed diagnosis and inappropriate treatment. The *good news* is that depression is usually treatable and curable.

For most, **acceptance** is strongly present even from the beginning and becomes increasingly dominant as time passes. Contrary to the other reactions that peak and then trend downward, **acceptance** moves steadily upward.

Complicated Grief

Grief may be complicated because of an abnormal cause of death such as homicide or suicide, or because of other unusual circumstances surrounding the death, or because of a convoluted relationship with the decedent. *Complicated* grief can be distinguished from *normal* grief by the presence of severe grief reactions that persist at least twelve months in adults and six months in children following a death. It interferes with the capacity to function and increases the risk of serious mental and physical health issues.

In complicated grief, your life can seem like a ball of tangled-up Christmas tree light chords that you are struggling to unravel, and then you have to make sure all the bulbs are working. It's one of those times when professional help can *really* be helpful.

If you feel complicated grief (also referred to as Persistent Complex Bereavement Disorder) might apply to you, know that the standard for diagnosis and treatment is complex. It deals with reactive distress to the death, social/identity disruption, and possibly the traumatic nature of the death. Seek professional bereavement counseling to help get unstuck and to avoid prolonged distress.

Effects of Grief/Distress

Stress and anxiety are byproducts of grief and can overwhelm coping mechanisms and functionality, resulting in a feeling of helplessness. Some stress in life is unavoidable regardless of circumstances or conditions. In fact, the absence of stress/anxiety is death.

Like good and bad cholesterol (HDL and LDL), there is good and bad stress. *Good* stress (*eustress*) is healthy stimulation that motivates us in a positive way to accomplish things and to survive. *Bad* stress (*distress*) is excessive emotional pain and can diminish our ability to function, concentrate, and live. Add to this that grief-produced stress is usually accompanied by other stressors, which together can cause your brain and body to suffer.

Eustress is important because love, family, and social relationships can be affected. Long-term distress can lead to health problems including chronic fatigue, depression, heart disease, muscle aches, high blood pressure, and decreased immune function.

We vary in emotional endurance and resilience. Be accepting and understanding of those with greater or lesser degrees of these attributes. Variances are caused by factors such as culture, spirituality, age of the decedent, relationship with the decedent, cause of death, circumstances surrounding the death, secondary losses, and other concurrent crises. Sensitization *or* desensitization can also result from past exposures.

You may experience adverse physical, cognitive, emotional, behavioral and spiritual reactions. Traumatic distress causes sensory encoding that can result in flashbacks, nightmares, and delayed expressions—feelings surfacing sometime after the loss.

Normal reactions may include fatigue, insomnia, change in appetite, anxiety, crying, guilt, sadness, confusion, anger, withdrawal, the inability to concentrate and function well, and a challenge to your belief system.

On rare occasions a survivor may become suicidal. If you experience this, ***please ask yourself,*** "Do I really want to kill myself, or do I want a different life?" *When everything is coming at you, you're in the wrong lane.* Change lanes and get help! Don't give up! **YOU CAN HAVE HOPE!**

If at the brink of suicide, call the National Suicide Prevention Lifeline at 800-273-TALK (8255) or text the Crisis Text Line. Just text 741741 from your smart phone. Call 911 for local help. These are free services available 24/7.

Understand that depression is generally underrated and undertreated. Reluctance to acknowledge depression and seek treatment is a formula for continued misery and health issues. Talk therapy can give you a better understanding of what's going on and how to deal with it. Incidentally, depression is not a normal part of aging but may be associated with physical changes and medical conditions.

Management of Grief/Distress

An analogy of physiological disease might be helpful. The Centers for Disease Control define *disease* as the absence of effective antibodies, not the presence of a toxic environment. This suggests that increasing our ability (emotional "antibodies") to *manage* poignant grief is more effective than attempting to minimize or ignore it.

Initially, *walk toward* the pain for gradual desensitization. Confront emotional pain by accepting it. It is healthy and okay to cry. Tears help relieve distress. Trying to be macho by concealing or ignoring grief is ineffective and will merely prolong it.

After emotions stabilize, talk about what bothers you. Talk to those who will listen non-judgmentally. Talking about it can be difficult, but it helps to flush out pain. By doing so, you are likely to eat better, sleep better, remain healthier, and reduce disruption in your home and work life.

For example, talk about what you miss the most about your loved one. What is the worst thing about this for you now?

Talk about these things *repeatedly* for desensitization, and let family and friends know you need to do this.

The ability to talk about it indicates the ability to manage it. The more you talk about your loved one and how you feel, the easier it becomes. *That's the goal!* It's that simple (and that complicated). If other stressors are also affecting you, bring them up too. They can be aggravated by current grief and may need to be resolved for a better present life.

It is not unusual for survivors to experience some physical illness during the first six months of bereavement. Regular physical activity such as brisk walking, aerobics, swimming, bicycling, and some deep breathing, help to cope with distress. Alternate exercise with relaxation and mourning with happiness. *Balance* is a key word in life.

Pause occasionally to enjoy simple contemplative pleasures—"smell the roses." Listen to music, read a book, go to a concert or ball game, attend church, and enjoy life. Finding happiness reduces hypertension and is heart healthy. Isn't that what your loved one would want for you?

Love lives on as you move on. Discontinue unhealthy activities such as smoking, drug abuse, binge eating and/or binge drinking, being physically inactive, or attempting an emotional escape by spending too much time texting, or on the computer and internet, or over watching TV. These abnormalities delay recovery. Also, too much time in a virtual world can blur our *real*-world life.

Emotional trauma can create comorbidity with addictions by making instant gratification very appealing. Attempting to subdue sorrows with alcohol is a huge mistake. It will have the opposite effect! When you are depressed, alcohol becomes a depressant. When the momentary blur wears off, you will feel much worse. Using alcohol to medicate emotional distress is like pouring gasoline on a fire.

Alcoholics beware that only about 2% recover on their own. It is generally necessary to enter rehab for approximately thirty days.

What about prescribed mood medication to treat depression? If a chemical (rather than circumstantial) condition is causing or contributing to depression, medication may be in order. An *indication* of chemical causation is that some of the same symptoms existed prior to your loss. Determination can require differential diagnosis.

A study by Mark Tyrrell, Creative Director of *Uncommon Knowledge*, indicates, "Thyroid problems, food intolerances, and other physical illness can lead to feelings of depression, but less than ten percent of clinical depression is thought to have a chemical basis. Appropriate psychotherapy has still been shown to be more effective than drug treatment alone in the treatment of chemically based depression, and far more effective in preventing relapse."

Meds may be needed in the short-term if you are experiencing *extreme* complicated grief. Evidence is lacking, however, to suggest the use of meds for normal bereavement. Avoid suppression of grief. You need to go through it to get through it.

Medication may be a chemical pathway to feeling better. "Happy pills," however, do not deal with underlying causation and thus can impede real emotional recovery, prolong the grief process, and become habit forming. Meds may also have unpleasant side effects and mask the real cause of grief and depression.

From time to time, you may find solace in talking to the decedent even though you do not receive an audible response. Whether this is fantasy, or the decedent really hears you, we simply don't know. Someday on the other side, we shall gain an understanding of "paranormal activity." In the meantime, if it provides comfort and a sense of presence, *do* it.

Traumatic and treasured memories do not erode like everyday memories. As the frequency and severity of emotional pain diminishes over time, your loved one and the past will be preserved in your thoughts. You may occasionally re-experience your loss by unpleasant imaginal intrusion. Avoid addiction to this. Focus on *endearing* memories that can become enduring memories.

Precious memories can help sustain you through rough emotional terrain and make you a stronger, better person. For years, things like holidays, anniversaries, birthdays, or just talking about him or her may trigger treasured memories—*like having roses in December.*

You may hesitate to say goodbye to grief after it has become familiar to you, or because it might seem like you are abandoning your loved one. Don't fall in love with sorrow or build a shrine to grief.

At some point allow yourself to arrive at the end of your painful journey so you can begin the rest of your life. Let the darkness become light. Accepting the finality of your loved one's death is *not* forgetting your loved one. ***Completed grief* is when you can think about your loved one with *peace* instead of *pain*.**

For a very few, grief may never be completely healed. This can be compared to being born with a permanent disability such as blindness or missing a limb. You must adapt to make the best of it. A bereavement counselor can help with adaptation.

Self-care of Emotions

Emotional trauma needs relationships—not just dogma—to heal. Like the resting place for raindrops, so is the resting place for emotional trauma in the community. At the same time, there are helpful things *you can do for yourself.*

Only you can determine the pace and extent of painful emotional withdrawal from the deceased. Some remain emotionally connected; others eventually let go to move on. There is not necessarily a right or wrong.

Past painful experiences can intrude into the present as perceived threats. There is no permanent inoculation for this. However, there are things you can do to facilitate relaxation and calmness.

For example, if you want to relax in the presence of emotional stressors, relax your pelvic floor muscles. Those are the muscles that surround the bones you sit on. Don't flex and squeeze your buttocks together like you instinctively would if suddenly alarmed or tensed. Deliberately let them go totally unclenched and limp.

This interacts with two functional sections of your nervous system to help you relax. You have a *Sympathetic Nervous System* (SNS)—for "fight or flight," and a *Parasympathetic Nervous System* (PNS)—for "rest and digest." They function in opposition to each other.

Increasing one decreases the other. Relaxing your pelvic floor muscles supports the PNS.

The SNS is an *accelerator,* increasing metabolism, stress hormones, heart rate, respiratory rate and pupil dilation. PNS is a *break,* slowing metabolism, heart rate, and respiratory rate.

It is a technique used in sports such as football. For example, when a well-trained quarterback takes a snap, drops back to pass without finding an open receiver, sees a three-hundred-pound tackle coming full speed at him, and knows he's going to get hit, what does he do?

If he tenses and braces for the hit, the likelihood of getting hurt or possibly injured increases. Instead, he relaxes his pelvic floor muscles and lets his body become limp. The quarterback may go down and get bruised, but injury is less likely. He gets up ready for the next snap.

Resiliency and relaxation go hand in hand. We've all heard stories of a drunk driver who survives a horrible auto accident, uninjured, that might have killed someone else. Now you know why.

When confronted by stressors, other techniques while relaxing your pelvic floor muscles, include folding your hands behind your head, pulling your elbows back to stretch your chest, and breathing deeply.

Also, try humming simple familiar tunes like, "Happy Birthday" or "Row, Row, Row Your Boat" or a favorite hymn. This may seem silly, but try it! Momentarily disconnect from life's activities. I like to hum "Amazing Grace."

Death of a Spouse/Significant Other

When your spouse dies, it can seem like part of you is gone. Life will not be the same, nor can it be. If your spouse predeceased you, he or she was spared the emotional trauma you may be experiencing. This can provide a sense of relief for you and would be a *sign of your supreme love for him* or *her—the real deal!*

You may need to assume new and possibly unfamiliar responsibilities at a time when your ability to focus and concentrate is not up to par. At least temporarily, ask for help. Beware that there may be those who try to take advantage of you. Avoid added distress by observing the following.

If you are a young adult, suddenly some may seem overly helpful, friendly, and they want to hang out with you. Their motives might be inappropriate and poorly timed.

If you sense this, decline their further assistance and let them know you need some space. It is easy to be vulnerable when distraught. Be strong and on guard. Stand your ground!

Starting a new intimate relationship before being mentally and emotionally ready can be disastrous. It is best to avoid this for at least a year. A new spouse will need assurances that he or she is number one in your life. The spouse will not want to hear a lot about (or be compared to) the one you lost.

The next spouse (if any) will be different and have idiosyncrasies (and possibly eccentricities) that may not be a good long-term fit for you. Don't get involved in dating until the desire becomes constant, bereavement has been completed, and you know you are *really* ready. **Remember this:** where the honey is, there are the bees also.

If you are a senior citizen having to take over unfamiliar financial and business matters, it may be very helpful to seek help from someone trustworthy and capable. Beware that scam artists consider you easy prey. Mailings, emails and phone calls from fraudulent "charities" and other scammers hit seniors the hardest.

Death of a Child

I've met with parents whose children have predeceased them. They will often tearfully say, "I'm not supposed to outlive my children!" This is heartbreaking regardless of the son's or daughter's age.

If your child died recently and was living with you, it is suggested that you leave his or her things intact for a while to provide a sense of presence and avoid exacerbating an overwhelming emotional emptiness.

If additional children come along, don't suppress the knowledge of their predecessor's death. Be open about it, and answer their questions while they are young.

Avoid trying to make substitutes (replacement children) out of siblings or future children. Each child is a unique person and needs to carve out his or her own identity and legacy.

Each parent is also unique. Don't expect your spouse or the other parent to handle grief exactly as you do. Male/female distinctions and the relationship each had with the child and with each other contribute to differing coping styles.

Be understanding and forgiving to avoid relational strains. Share your thoughts, feelings, and needs with the other parent and family members. Ask them how they are doing. Sometimes the death of a child can reconnect estranged parents and family members, or it can cause them to drift apart. Be careful.

It is best to wait a year or so before trying to have another child. Otherwise, if the grief process has not reached a sense of completion, it can keep returning as unfinished emotional business.

Caring for Grieving Young Children

Young children may seem slow in comprehending that a family member has died. Initially, tears may be momentarily delayed. This is because death is somewhat mysterious to them. They often repeat questions. It is how they learn and process things. Their feelings may be expressed behaviorally. Keep in mind that children do childish things. Good grief management can help these things trend in a positive direction.

Death should be explained to them in simple, honest, straightforward literal terms. They need to breathe the air of truth—no deception or shading. Don't make them feel isolated by avoiding the subject. Share thoughts and tears with them. Avoid saying things like, "God wanted him in heaven." This can cause resentment toward God. "You are now the man of the house." This can cause an unnecessary burden at an inappropriate time.

Provide paper and crayons for young children to draw and color pictures. This can be therapeutic for them and give adults an idea of what might be on their minds. Their drawings may indicate denial or fantasy. Happy, sad, or angry emotions may be illustrated. Don't be critical of a reality disassociation. Let them feel free to act out their grief.

Give them assurances that they are loved and will be cared for. Children should be encouraged (*but not forced*) to talk about how they feel and what they think about the death. They need to know they have permission to do so. It is a crucial time in their development. While struggling to understand what happened, and to sort out how they should react, they may become sullen.

Parents, guardians and relatives can be good role models by grieving openly and sharing memories with the children. Look at family photos and watch family videos together. Death and the decedent's absence are difficult to discuss, but it will help you and the children get through a difficult time. An open and healthy bereavement process is an aid to good functionality and development into adolescence and adulthood.

Child-rearing tip: *Be a warm but firm coach*! **Warm:** With great affection remind them frequently how much you love them. Give them lots of hugs. Spend time with them. Take them places *they* enjoy. **Firm:** Be strict and do not put up with misbehavior. Listen to them and avoid *over* lecturing.

Evaluate their significant experiences with them. *Unevaluated* experience does not improve anyone. Spend enough *quality time* with them so they *know* they are priorities in your life. Do not put this off and experience regrets later. Their first eight years are the most formative. You do not want your children emotionally scarred by reactive attachment disorder caused by interruptions in the bonding cycle.

As they approach their latter teen-age years, gradually transition from *coach* to *cheerleader*. Their dependency needs to begin evolving into *independence* by doing less and less for them because you love them more and more. This may be difficult, but it can play an important role in their future success. Learning to manage difficulties can be character building.

Caring for Grieving Teenagers

Teenagers in grief can gain a maturity level not often shared by their cohorts. They typically avoid expressing emotions openly. Don't assume a lack of grief. They feel things deeply but may be inclined to focus on the needs of others. At this time of their life, developmental challenges and uncertainties can have an effect. Be aware that some may be inclined to use drugs for emotional medication, delaying healing of distress.

If you are a teenager's parent (or old enough to be one), do not expect the teenager to think or feel at your maturity level. Show respect and have a mutual exchange of thoughts and concerns.

Children and teenagers tend to be resilient, but beware that they are also malleable, that is, capable of being shaped or adaptable by how they are treated and by their surroundings. Girls generally mature into adults in their early to mid-twenties and boys in their mid to late twenties.

If a teenager (or anyone else for that matter) seems reluctant to converse, try indirect probes such as, "You must miss him a lot" or "This must be hard for you." Provide assurances that it's okay to grieve openly, but don't force it.

Twenty-Five Best Coping Practices

There's an old adage "If you keep doing what you're doing, you'll keep getting what you're getting"—positively or negatively. Sometimes an adjustment of priorities is necessary. Select those practices below that fit you and that you are ready for now—not too many at one time. Take it one day at a time. Be positive and avoid excuses. Be patient but keep nudging yourself along.

1. *Walk toward the pain.* Don't subdue it; go through it. It's the only way out. Ignoring or masking the grief prolongs distress.

2. Avoid trying to be macho. Concealing reality restrains recovery.

3. Crying is healthy and okay. Let your feelings show honestly.

4. Don't be in a hurry to remove your loved one's belongings. They can provide a sense of presence. Don't allow others to control this.

5. View your loved one's photos, videos, and endearing keepsakes. Focus on his or her life rather than the death. Remember with joy more than sadness, and remember that a picture can be worth a thousand words.

6. Journalize your thoughts, emotions, and reactions. This can be a release valve. It also becomes therapeutic when you share it with others.

7. Sometimes, it is comforting to talk to your loved one even though there is no audible response. It can provide a sense of presence. What would your loved one say to you if he or she were with you now?

8. Occasionally, compose a letter to your loved one. They can be very impactful, especially when read at the gravesite or near the ashes or where the death occurred. They can also become comforting mementos.

9. Rituals such as lighting a candle or planting a memorial tree can be consoling reminders.

10. Take care of yourself physically. Get enough sleep and eat nutritious meals high in carbohydrates and low in sugar.

11. Avoid excessive use of caffeine—a blood pressure elevator.

12. Do not use alcohol or unprescribed drugs to medicate emotional pain! When depressed, drugs and alcohol act as depressants. They may provide a momentary blur, but afterwards, the depression shall return with a vengeance—like pouring gasoline on a fire!

13. Exercise. Aerobics and walking are excellent to help manage adrenalin. Breathe deeply and relax your pelvic floor muscles. (See the "Self-Care of Emotions" section) Alternate exercise and relaxation.

14. Forgive yourself for all the things you believe you should have said or done. Avoid critiquing and blaming yourself.

15. Avoid feeling guilty that you are still alive. Be kind to yourself.

16. Avoid isolation, especially on holidays, birthdays, anniversaries, and other special days for a while.

17. Spend time with others. Socialize often.

18. Tell and retell what is bothering you the most until it is no longer bothering you the most.

19. Seek help and accept offered help. People do care and want to help.

20. Put off major life changes for at least a year if possible.

21. Keep busy and focused. Idleness can produce morbidity.

22. Reframe your life. Remember with love instead of pain; take hold of peace and a new life gain. Love lasts beyond grief through a commitment to living again. It's okay to be happy and these honors your loved one. Death ends a life, but there is a sense in which your loved one remains with you.

23. Welcome back a sense of purpose. Reevaluate your life and invest in it. Take hold of the future and reassess your goals and plans. Start with small goals, and work your way up. Bereavement should reach a *positive* turning point. It is not too late to seek a better world.

24. Indulge yourself by doing things you enjoy. Get out and have some fun. Reignite happiness and enjoyment in life!

25. If you are struggling with anxiety, depression, and functional disruption, a couple of years after death, *complicated grief* may be indicated. Have a professional assess your coping and help you avoid further derailment.

A New Day Dawning

It is important for you to pick a day to begin a new epoch! The term *epoch* means more than a mere period of time. It is a period marked by something uniquely or highly significant—a memorable development. When grief is completed, and you are ready, *pick a day.* Make a note of it, make your loved one proud, and let the new epoch begin.

A statement by British poet, Alfred, Lord Tennyson, 1809-1892, may have meaning for you. **"How dull it is to pause, to make an end, to rust unburnished, not to shine in use!"**

You may find it rewarding to get involved helping others who have lost a loved one in death. As a peer, your words of encouragement could be respected and appreciated. The nurturing of others and the pride of accomplishment can be meaningful to you as well.

Grief/Bereavement Counseling

When recovering from a *physical injury*, sometimes we need physical therapy to help us return to normal functioning. The same is true for *emotional* injury caused by bereavement. We have to relearn not only how to live, but also how to live above grief. Emotional therapy through individual and/or group counseling can make it easier. Counseling is a must for grief that won't resolve. When distressed, dealing with grief on your own can be like trying to send email without Wi-Fi.

Counseling is best within the first year of bereavement but can be quite helpful long after that. Avoidance of counseling may result in the development of an inappropriate coping system that not only fails to reach best results but also becomes problematic over time.

Have realistic expectations of how counseling can help you. Do not expect to leave a counseling session and find that everything will be just fine from then on. Following a plan is necessary, and a time element is unavoidable.

Do expect to receive answers, information and techniques that can help you *personally* get through a difficult time and accelerate emotional recovery. You don't need to feel like you're sailing against the wind or moving through quicksand.

Most recover on their own, but it can be more difficult and take longer. Those with significant physical, social, occupational, or speaking impairments may be at risk without counseling. Issues existing prior to the death can exacerbate grief and increase the need for professional evaluation and treatment.

If you have a history of depression, or you are dealing with additional stressors, or you lost a spouse, child, or sibling, or your loved one died in an unusual manner—violence, homicide, suicide, or an accident—counseling can be very beneficial. *You are strongest when you seek help.* It is a sign of wisdom, *not* weakness.

Individual and/or group confidential counseling sessions are safe places to express your grief and have it validated. Each type of session takes about one to two hours and each has specific advantages.

Individual sessions provide a comfortable setting for an emotional release by talking one-on-one with an empathetic listener. An educational component is included to help you gain a deeper understanding of your personal grief and stress. The goal is to develop a *specific plan* for you to live above grief.

Group sessions provide the advantage of being with peers. You discover that you are not the only one going through what you are going through, and that you are experiencing *normal* reactions to an *abnormal* event. It can be a time of mutual support and bonding.

Regular attendance at group sessions can help you stay on track as your emotional pain enters remission. How long should you keep attending? Continue as long as you feel the need.

Faith—for the Best of Hope
In the Worst of Times

Sir Thomas More (1478-1535) wrote, "Earth hath no sorrows that heaven cannot heal." Dealing with spirituality is part of treating the whole person. Body, mind and spirit lean on each other for healing and care.

Experience shows that people of spiritual faith generally have greater success dealing with grief/distress. A lack of faith raises the likelihood of experiencing prolonged struggles with anger, bitterness and depression. Faith can detoxify those negatives. *For some it is the only thing that works.*

If you lack a spiritual connection, this is an opportune time to discontinue meandering through life without a personal relationship with God. Following is a presentation of genuine Christianity. If you embrace a non-Christian religion, you may want to stop here. You are invited, however, to continue and consider.

The legendary theologian, Karl Barth (1886-1968), was once asked by a student, "Dr. Barth, what is the most profound thought you ever had?" Without hesitation, his response was a quote from a children's song, "Jesus loves me this I know, for the Bible tells me so...." Pope Pius XII described Karl Barth as the most important theologian since Thomas Aquinas (1225-1274).

The best of hope in the worst of times is not found in "religion" per se. *Religion* is mankind's attempt to live at peace in a difficult situation. It is not necessarily a genuine quest for God. Religion involves asceticism: rituals, rules, regulations, and taboos. These can result in hypocrisy and inordinate self-esteem. There are many man-made religions and gods. *God created man, and man returned the favor.*

Real Christianity is *really* not a religion. In fact, when Christ walked on Earth, His chief enemies were the religious leaders. **The distinctive feature of genuine Christianity is that God takes the initiative, sometimes through blessing, and sometimes through adversity ultimately leading to blessing.**

Salvation (how we get to heaven) is summarized in the most familiar Bible verse, John 3:16, "For God so loved the world that He gave His only begotten Son, that whoever believes in Him should not perish, but have eternal life.*" Every requirement to enter heaven is there!*

The Bible explains further, "For all have sinned and fall short of the glory of God..." (Romans 3:23), and "...the wages of sin is death, but the gift of God is eternal life in Jesus Christ our Lord" (Romans 6:23). Our salvation is succinctly stated in Ephesians 2:8-9, "For by grace you have been saved through faith; and that not of yourselves; it is the gift of God; not as a result of works, so that no one may boast." In other words, we cannot earn our salvation. That's why it's called a "Gift of God," *paid for, in full, by the blood of Christ.*

God's ***grace*** is everything for nothing to those who don't deserve anything. No matter what's in our past or future, His grace is infinitely greater than all our sins. ***Faith*** is described in Hebrews 11:1, as follows, "Now faith is the assurance of things hoped for, the conviction of things not seen." ***Saving faith*** means to so trust Jesus Christ, that if anything else was necessary, we would not be admitted into heaven.

Jesus confirmed that there is no other way by declaring, "I am the way, and the truth, and the life; no one comes to the Father, but through Me" (John 14:6). The resurrection of Jesus is a provable fact that confirms who He was and what He said.

"Therefore, since we have been justified by faith, we have peace with God through our Lord Jesus Christ. Through him we have also obtained access by faith into this grace in which we stand, and we rejoice in hope of the glory of God" (Romans 5:1-2). *If death were no more than the lights going out, this really wouldn't matter so much.*

Some become believers in their final moments, *like the thief who was dying on a cross next to the cross of Jesus* (Luke 23:39-43). The thief said to Him, "Lord, remember me when You come into your kingdom." Jesus responded, "Assuredly, I say to you, today you will be with Me in Paradise."

If you are not sure where you stand with God, you can be! A personal relationship with the Lord and a home in heaven can be secured by praying a simple prayer like: "God, I acknowledge that I am a sinner and that I will accept Jesus as my personal Savior. Thank you for loving me, for forgiveness and for the *gift* of eternal life. Amen." **If you have never come to faith in Christ, or you are uncertain, pray that prayer *now*.**

Once you've prayed a prayer like that, you are as ready and fit for heaven as you'll ever be. You are born anew. A hopeless end becomes an endless hope. "Therefore, if any man is in Christ, he is a new creation; the old things are passed away; behold, new things have come" (2 Corinthians 5:17).

As believers, God begins to radically change our lives, and though we all stray at times, we never recover from having become a "new creation." 1 Peter 1:4-5 tells us that we have a guaranteed reservation in heaven and that we are kept by the power of God, and He never has a power outage.

If you are a parent, you know there is nothing you, nor any child of yours, can do to end the biological parent/child relationship. The fellowship and enjoyment, however, can be affected by obedience or disobedience. The relationship we have with our Heavenly Father works in a similar way.

By the way, if a child dies before reaching an age of accountability (being able to understand grace and forgiveness through Christ), he or she is safe and will spend eternity in heaven (2 Samuel 12:22-23).

Three things to help you *grow in grace*: (1) Read the Bible and accept it at face value. It is the only *absolute* authority for doctrine and practice. (2) Pray. (3) Get involved in a Bible teaching church.

These things nourish and strengthen our spiritual life. The first two should be done daily. Share your faith with others. God does not work in a vacuum; He works through us. Imagine that!

The Gospel of John (fourth book in the New Testament) is a good place to begin reading—profound thought in simple words. Bible translations with a penchant for accuracy and readability include the New King James Version (NKJV, Second Edition, 2007), the New American Standard Bible (NASB 1995), the English Standard Version (ESV copyrighted in 2001), and the Holman Christian Standard Bible, 2009. They are also available as study Bibles having explanatory notes. Check with local or on-line Bible bookstores. Other bookstores may also carry these, Bibles.

Sample Scriptures for Stressful Seasons

Healing for the heart by an awesome God: Psalm 147:3-5
> He heals the brokenhearted, and binds
> [*bandages*] up their wounds [*sorrows*].
> He counts the number of the stars; He gives names to all of
> them.
> Great is our Lord, and abundant in strength; His understanding
> is infinite.

*[There are upwards of a trillion galaxies, each containing from about
ten million to a hundred trillion stars. Now read the above again.]*

**Joy and peace surpassing human understanding:
Philippians 4:4-7**
> Rejoice in the Lord always. Again, I will say, rejoice! Let your
> gentleness [calmness] be known to all men. The Lord is at
> hand. Be anxious for nothing, but in everything by prayer
> and supplication, with thanksgiving, let your requests be
> made known to God. And the peace of God, which surpasses
> all understanding, will guard your hearts and minds through
> Christ Jesus.

*[When the apostle Paul penned the above words, he was a prisoner in a
Roman jail because of his faith—not a fun place to be!]*

An eternal home for believers: John 14:1-4
> Let not your heart be troubled; you believe in God, believe
> also in Me. In My Father's house are many mansions; if it
> were not so, I would have told you. I will go to prepare a
> place for you. And if I go and prepare a place for you, I will
> come again and receive you to Myself; that where I am, *there*

you may be also. And where I go you know, and the way you know.

Grief and anxiety replaced by hope and comfort: 1 Thessalonians 4:13-18

We do not want you to be uninformed, brothers, concerning those who are asleep [*deceased*], so that you will not grieve like the rest [*in the same way*], who have no hope. Since we believe that Jesus died and rose again, in the same way God will bring with Him those who have fallen asleep through Jesus.

For this we say to you by a revelation of the Lord: We who are still alive at the Lord's coming will have no advantage over those who have fallen asleep. For the Lord Himself will descend from heaven with a shout, with the archangel's voice and with the trumpet of God, and the dead in Christ will rise first. Then we who are still alive will be caught up together with them in the clouds to meet the Lord in the air and so we will always be with the Lord. Therefore, encourage one another with these words.

[In the above verses, you see the word "asleep" a few times. In the original Greek, it is a very gentle word that could depict a baby having been rocked to sleep. It is also used to describe believers who have died—even the martyr Stephen who was stoned to death in Acts chapter 7. This word is never used for the death of unbelievers or the death of Jesus. Jesus died a violent death for us.]

A living hope, inheritance and reservation: 1 Peter 1:3-5

Blessed be the God and Father of our Lord Jesus Christ, who according to His great mercy has caused us to be born again to a living hope through the resurrection of Jesus Christ from the dead, to obtain an inheritance which is imperishable and undefiled and will not fade away, reserved in heaven for you, who are protected by the power of God through faith for a salvation ready to be revealed in the last time.

Faith and peace triumph over tribulation: Romans 5:1-5

Therefore, having been justified by faith, we have peace with God through our Lord Jesus Christ, through whom also we have access by faith into this grace in which we stand, and rejoice in hope of the glory of God. And not only that, but we also glory in tribulations, knowing that tribulation produces perseverance; and perseverance, character; and character, hope. Now hope does not disappoint, because the love of God has been poured out in our hearts by the Holy Spirit who was given to us.

Life after the end of time: Revelation 21:1-6

Now I saw a new heaven and a new earth, for the first heaven and the first earth had passed away. Also, there was no more sea. Then I, John, saw the holy city, new Jerusalem, coming down out of heaven from God, prepared as a bride adorned for her husband.

And I heard a loud voice from heaven saying, "Behold, the tabernacle of God is with men, and He will dwell with them, and they shall be His people. God Himself will be with them, and be their God. And God will wipe away every tear from their eyes; there shall be no more death, nor sorrow, nor crying. There shall be no more pain, for the former things have passed away." Then He who sat on the throne said, "Behold, I make all things new." And He said to me, "Write, for these words are true and faithful." And He said to me, "It is done! I am the Alpha and the Omega, the Beginning and the End. I will give of the fountain of the water of life freely to him who thirsts.

[The New Testament was originally written in Greek. "Alpha" and "Omega" are the first and last letters of the Greek alphabet.}

We cannot begin to imagine all the glories and wonders of heaven our Lord has prepared for believers. When we enter heaven, I suspect we may gasp in awe and have an *"Oh my God!"* moment—joy and peace—like never before and forevermore!

We may be disappointed by how little we have done for Jesus, but one of our greatest joys will be how much He has done for us.

The Bible concludes with a prayer by the apostle John: "Even so, come, Lord Jesus! The grace of our Lord Jesus Christ be with you all. Amen."

Notes and Memories